ASHLEE CRAFT /
ASSEMBLAGE

ISSUE 14
FEBRUARY 11, 2019

by Ashlee Craft

1

Published by Freedom Meadow Media

Top half of cover photo by Ashlee Craft; bottom half public domain image

ISBN: 9781091500303

TABLE OF CONTENTS

A LETTER FROM LE EDITOR

Pivoting. Changing course. Realizing
that the shit you were doing wasn't
painting rainbows on your walls for you
anymore so you left it behind.

I know it's been a long time since the
weird + the wonderful *Assemblage* has
shown its New Issue face. And everything
is shifting. Still shifting. So much has
changed since the last issue. I feel
like I'm almost literally a whole new
person now. Theoretically, I probably am
(your whole body is built anew at least
once every few years with cells dying &
being reborn, according to science). But
I sure feel it. This past year has
brought to me so many changes. Leaving
behind a job I fucking hated (leaving

from necessity, & also finally realizing
I DESERVED better & finally having the
balls to PURSUE "better"). Joining an
awesome personal development group which
exposed me to an environment of people
who were serious about making amazing
changes in their lives. And finally
towards the end of this year, just over
the past few months, finally beginning
to actually LIVE my life the way I've
always wanted to. Living from the place
of being worthy & of feeling good
consistently. Every fucking day. I've
began living each day in a way that's
perfect & as awesome as it can be. And
it feels SO FUCKING GOOD. Oh? And did I
mention that in 2018 I also FINALLY
FUCKING BEAT BOTH ALL MY DEPRESSION &
MOST OF MY ANXIETY???? How fucking cool
is that? You can read about that in this
Issue.

It's been, without a doubt, the BEST.
YEAR. OF. MY. LIFE.

There are so many projects I'm so
freaking excited to be working on. I'm
getting into standup comedy.
Interviewing amazing people. Doing weird
collaborations. Making freaking cool
music. I pivoted on what & how I write.
Making art that feels so inspired &
satisfying to make. I feel like I've
pivoted on almost everything. Feel like
I've been thirty-two different people

this year. And finally I am the best one.

Yes, *Assemblage* is coming back. It's bringing with it so many awesome art things & poetry & I can't wait to share it all with you. I'm thinking of the new incarnation of Assemblage as being a sort of book-format Patreon. You get to see samples of things I'm working on. You get to see the first glimpses of ideas I'm developing. You get the weird funky art that I know how to make now. That I'm letting myself make now. The real art.

Things are finally okay.

  - Ashlee Craft, Explorer of the World
    & brand-new Life Enthusiast

WHAT MIKE SAID

I saw them twice the first time I heard the song & I
remembered when I loved him & / I cleaned the office building
stone gray floors there were books on the shelf about NYC &
the bathroom was dark green / among file boxes my eyes
were filled with stars, dust & I felt warm inside when I
remembered how he looked at me / the second time I heard it I
raised my eyes up towards the clear open sky & the stars were
vibrant & on the breezy hill I remembered how I had to turn it
off before the temptation to do what never should be done
became too strong & I returned to almost being there & / all I
wanted was a way to numb away those feelings but I sat on
the hill knowing fully what I had overcome & I remembered the
way he had looked at me & what it meant to me as I was lying
on the floor crying & it felt so good to know I no longer need
that

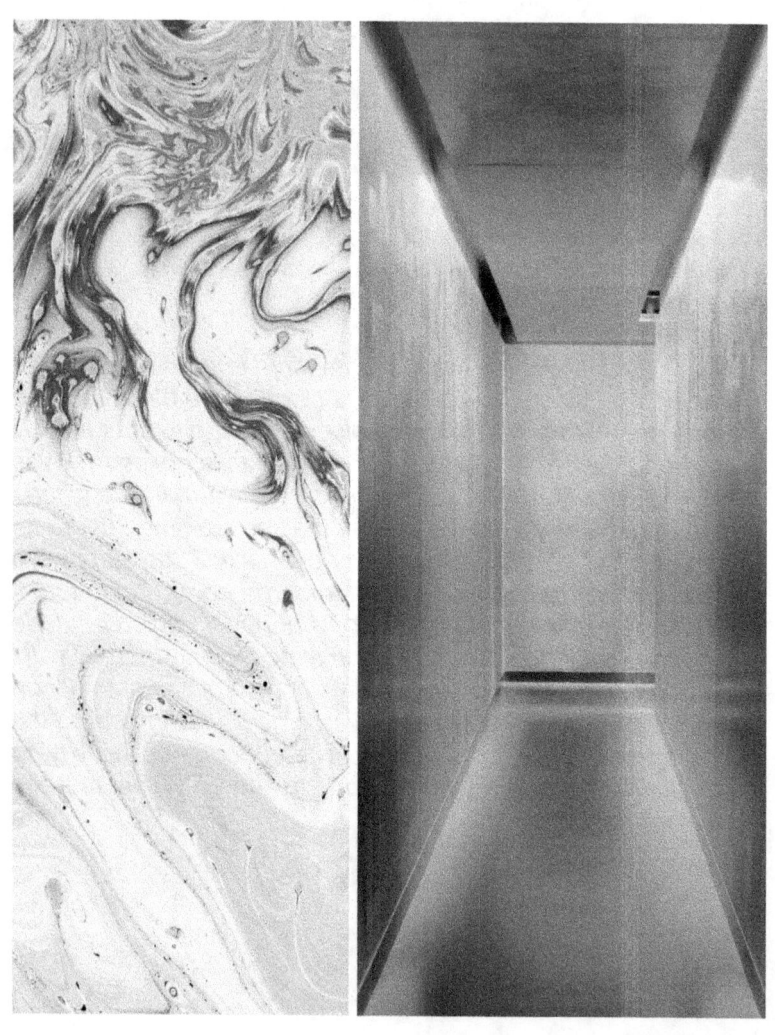

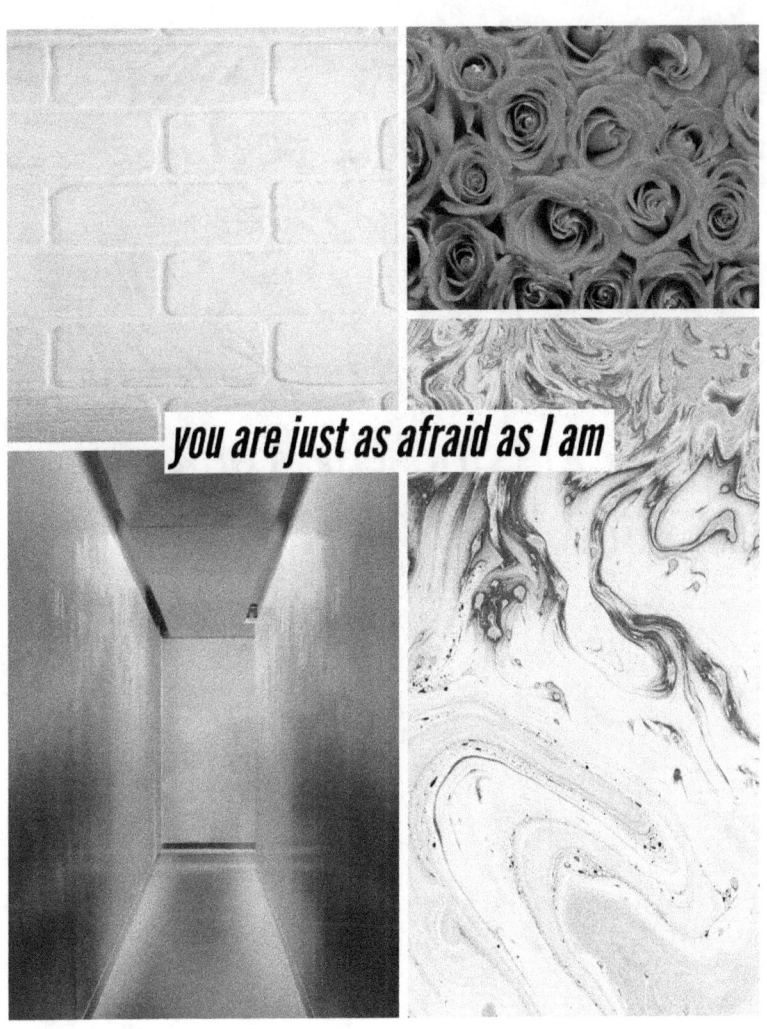

you are just as afraid as I am

you know what I feel like
doing right now?????

pushing you up against the
wall & kissing the fuck out
of you

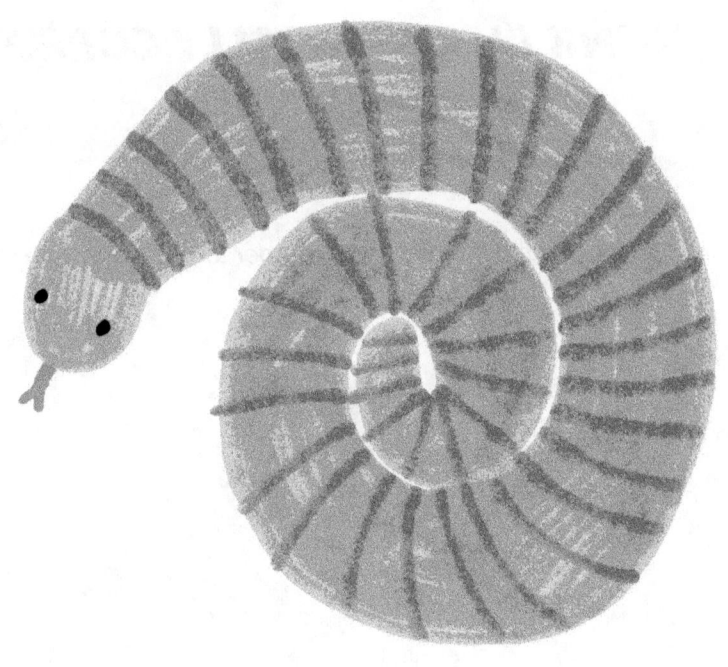

I THINK I HAVE FINALLY CURED MY DEPRESSION

by Ashlee Craft

I finally gathered the things I need in order to know how to thrive.

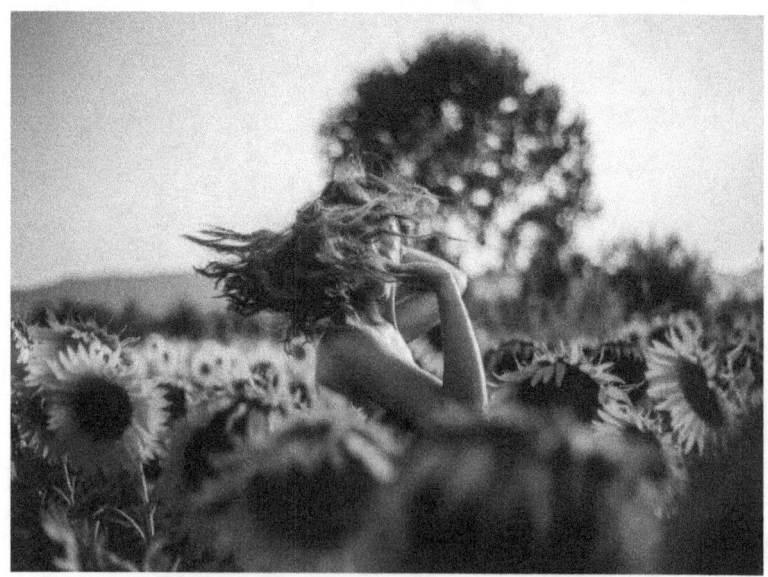

Photo by Matteo Vistocco **on** Unsplash

Originally published on The Ascent

I think I have finally cured my depression.

I have been depressed for ten years. And that is enough. And I think I've finally beat it.

Unlike other times I thought I had won, my healing was not due to willpower, or by forcing myself out of the darkness with willpower alone & convincing myself that I did indeed feel better.

Instead, everything changed because I changed my environment into one which allowed me to gather tools & learn how to use them & manipulate them into the things I needed to be. And most importantly, an environment that *let* me use them.

After almost a decade of being (never formally diagnosed, but I know how I've felt) clinically depressed, I finally feel like I've actually won. I've had my moments before of triumph, of discovering some secret that let me be happy for sometimes months at a time. But it was never like this before.

See, every time I felt "cured" before, I was always afraid that it was all in my head. That one day, the depression would come crashing back down on me. I never could believe that maybe I was actually cured. Because the other times, the feeling of "cured" had come about so suddenly that I usually couldn't see a logical reason for why I felt that way. Not to say that those times of being cured didn't mean anything, because they meant a great deal. It's just that they couldn't last because there was no concrete reason for WHY I felt cured.

And mostly it was because despite my "healing", I was still the exact same person inside. I was still just a depressed person experiencing happiness for a while.

But this time, it's different. And this time, I'm not afraid.

Because this time, my healing wasn't this sudden miracle that happened out of the blue. My healing was a slow, deliberate process. It's been a long time coming, but I feel like it finally might be here. And I feel like this time, it's going to last.

Why?

I have finally learned the tools & put systems in place that are necessary to keep myself happy. **I have built those tools & used those tools & figured out how to best make them work for me. I have molded those tools into systems & new actions & new ways of responding to life. I have built a solid foundation out of these tools. I have used these tools to become a different person.**

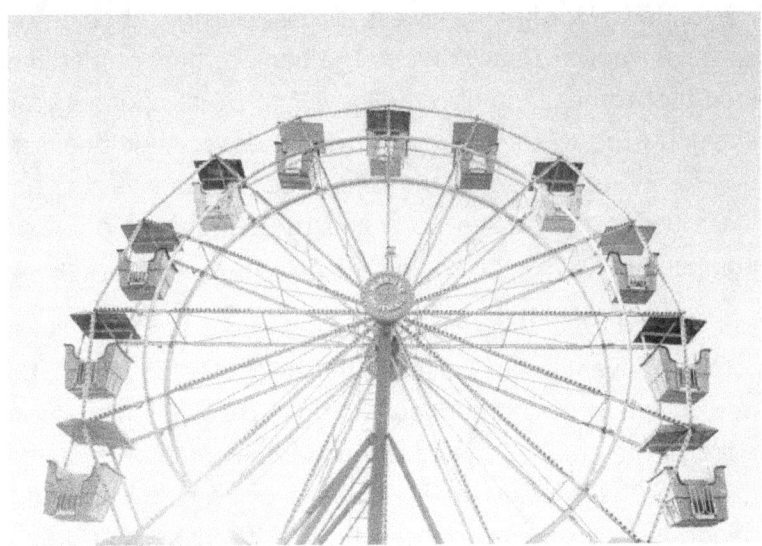

Photo by Hannah Morgan *on* Unsplash

This is why I believe my happiness foundation is stable now. It's didn't happen by magic; it happened by gathering & learning tools, & by using them.

Author & speaker Darren Hardy says that learning is the ability to produce a result. If you haven't produced the desired result, you haven't learned it yet.

Since January this year, I've been part of author Benjamin Hardy's outstanding AMP course (previously known as 52 Weeks of Momentum) & mentorship group. Thanks to being part of the group, I've read the most amazing combination of high-level books that I've read in any year, ever. My mind has linked together so many concepts between various books & I've had numerous breakthroughs that have utterly changed my life.

Benjamin Hardy's newest, best-selling book is called *Willpower Doesn't Work*. The book centers around the idea that rather than using willpower to try to change your life, you need to change your environment so that it causes you to naturally become the kind of person you need to be. Once you're the person you need to BE, you can do what you need to DO so you can have what you want to HAVE.

But the biggest thing this course has done for me was totally reinvent my mindset in the best way possible. The books I've read throughout the course, plus Benjamin Hardy's mentorship, the exceptional other members of the group, & the course content have taught me a whole new mindset, which I then applied to my life in brilliant ways. Brilliant, especially the ways I am finally understanding how to apply them to my life.

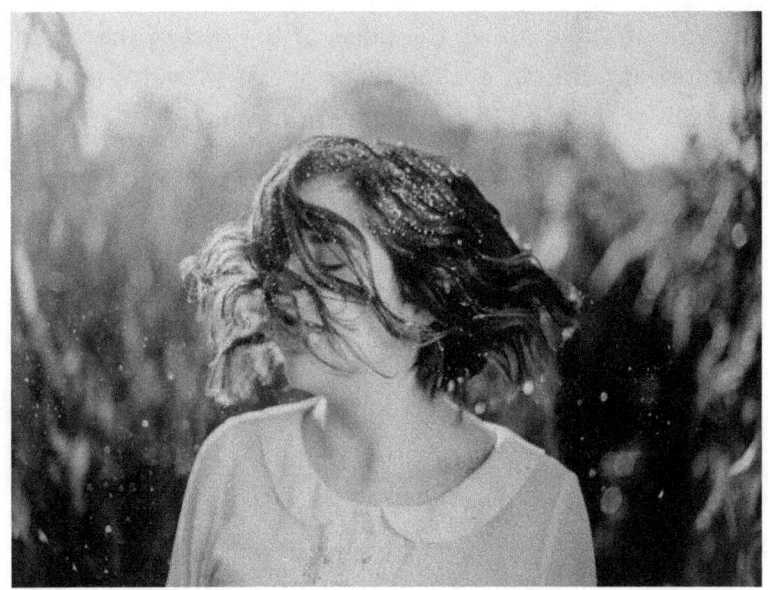

Photo by Hazzel Silva *on* Unsplash

In the middle of June, I had a huge mindset shift. Everything slowly began to change. I can't name a specific THING that changed it; the assemblage & combined influence of everything I was learning & experiencing & doing in all aspects of my life finally were mixing together in the perfect way.

And over the next two months, I made a lot of changes that shifted my mindset majorly. I started listening to podcasts & audiobooks in my car & at work whenever I could. I filled my mind with high-level stuff & surrounded myself with the environment & the people I needed to be around, to the best of my abilities. I committed to eating healthy & exercising. **I committed to living a life that I loved. I started committing to caring for myself & my goals first,** prioritizing them above the noise of the rest of the world. Because if I am not shining as bright as I can for myself, how am I supposed to be a light for others?

In the back of my mind, I guess I realized it. A lot of difficult things happened in the span of those two months, things that tested this new person I was becoming. But in the back of my mind, I still knew it was true.

I was slowly becoming less depressed. Slowly becoming deeply & unequivocally happy.

The sun rises slowly, & we still see darkness until we realize the sky has become light again. I didn't usually realize how the depression was fading & happiness was becoming a more predominant emotion until I *realized*.

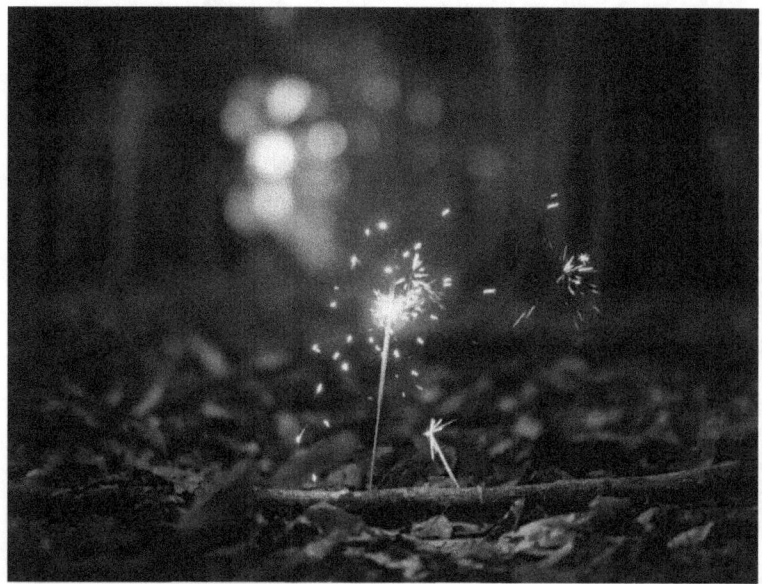

Photo by Jamie Street on Unsplash

It turns out, the environment I most needed to change was the environment inside me. And there I was, slowly & quietly chipping away at the darkness which had held me back for so long. Slowly building a better foundation, brick by brick.

Then the breakthrough happened. **And the foundation was suddenly recognizable as a *foundation*.**

I was listening to the audiobook version of the excellent book *Breaking the Habit of Being Yourself* by Dr. Joe Dispenza. It's one of the books we're reading for the 52 Weeks of Momentum course.

And I heard this phrase:

"[...] train the body to be the mind in order to live a predicable future based on a memory of a known past."

And he talks about how when something happens & you feel a certain way, your body remembers the way it feels, it keeps firing those neurons together until they wire together. If they fire & wire together for long enough, eventually the emotion from that singular incident can end up becoming your personality.

That's when I had my breakthrough.

All or at least most of my depression throughout the past decade most likely stemmed from my first bout of it that I experienced when I was 14.

At 14, the feelings of depression were new & interesting & mysterious. I reveled in them, wanted to explore them because I'd never quite felt that way before. I felt a sense of connection with others, even fictional characters, who felt that way. **So feeling depressed became a way of feeling connected to something bigger & more interesting than myself.**

And because that was my mindset, whenever something happened, I'd feel like it was a relevant time to feel depressed. Something along the lines of, "If I am a depressed person, this would be a time that I should feel depressed so I will look for those feelings of depression in this situation until I find them." So I replayed the feelings in my mind, felt depressed, & did it all over again.

I'm not saying none of my depression would have happened if it wouldn't have experienced that first episode & found it so interesting. I think it's likely I still would have experienced depression from time to time naturally due to fluctuations in brain chemistry. And I'm not saying what worked for me will necessarily help you feel better. But I'm sharing this here because I hope it helps someone. Because it helped me. And I want you to know it DOES get better.

I also want to note that my depression was fucking painful, difficult to deal with, & dangerous. I do not want anything I've said here to be construed as me saying that I "wasn't really depressed" because I WAS. I know how much of a struggle it was just to make it through each day for a VERY LONG TIME & how unrelenting & dark those feelings were. To claim I "wasn't depressed" because I was able to "cure" it is to get into the whole "more mentally ill than thou" mindset, which does

20

nothing but invalidate the very real experiences of people suffering from something, but perhaps not as badly as you are. This is harmful for everyone involved & only increases the stigma against mental illness because it causes people who should seek help to perhaps NOT seek help because they don't think they're "ill" enough to need/deserve help. Which is definitely harmful. I also want to note that while I consider myself "cured" & revel daily in how my life literally feels like a different life in a different world than how I used to feel, I still understand that if I fell back into my old mindset, habits, & lifestyle, that I would most likely feel the same way again. Me being "cured" means experiencing no symptoms, but it is still conditional upon me continuing the same healthy mindset, habits, goals, & worldview. It is my responsibility to keep myself feeling good.

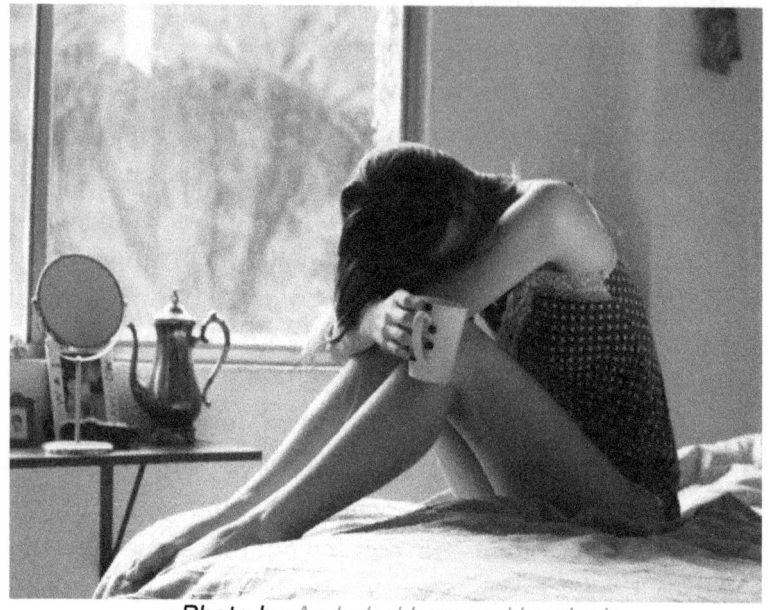

< Photo by Asdrubal luna on Unsplash

This cycle of feeling depressed & finding it interesting began to grow on its own. Out of my control. Then it wasn't so interesting anymore. Then it was something I had to struggle through. Something I had to fight off ferociously so that it would never succeed in its desperate efforts to push my head under the water & keep it there. Sometimes, it took everything I had to just to push it away one more time. It would retreat for a while, but hours or days or months later, there it would be again. It became darker & harder to control as it grew.

The depression became a big part of my personality. It became an addiction, in a way. I almost felt incomplete without it.

I tried feeling better. I used all the willpower I could muster up. Tried to force myself out of it. Pulled myself up by my bootstraps, time & time again. Sometimes I felt "cured". But like I said, I was still the same person inside. Still a depressed person deep down who was trying to be happy. I still didn't have any foundation in place to make the good feelings stick around.

Since the beginning of the year, I've really been trying. I've been learning. And I've been taking action on what I learned. But it was just over the past few weeks that it finally all *clicked*.

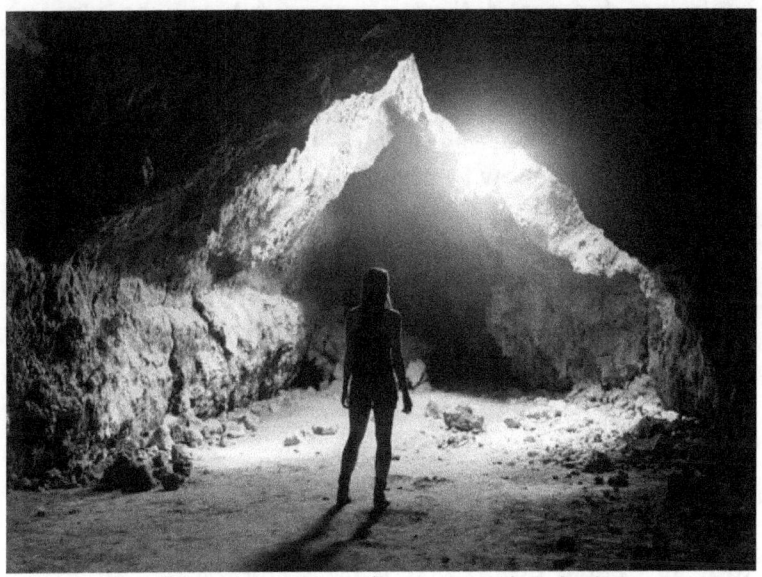

Photo by *Joshua Sortino* on *Unsplash*

Admittedly, I was afraid to move on from depression. Terrified to let go of it actually. Because after having it for so long, I was terrified that if I moved on from the

depressed feelings, I'd always feel like something was missing. That my art & my personality would be lame & one-note without it. That in the back of my mind, I would always be longing to feel those feelings again. Craving them.

But the quote from *Breaking the Habit of Being Yourself* not only showed me the cause of my often depression-based personality, but also why I was afraid of moving on from it.

A memory of the known past.

I was afraid to let myself be happy because I was so used to being depressed that a happy future was also an uncertain one. At least with my depression, I had its cold stale hand to hold, a familiarity I knew I could always return to. With depression, at least I knew what my future would feel like & how I would cope with it.

But once I realized both the cause of my depression & the reason it was terrifying to move away from it, it all became so flimsy, like a house of cards in the breeze.

And then all it became was something in my past. Not who I was anymore. Not who the future fated me to be.

I started being able to see myself as someone that a joyful, vibrant future was possible for, & I've never felt that so deeply before. I tear up a little bit as I write this, because five years ago, I never could have fathomed a future as full of possibility as the one I'm able to see now. Back then, it always seemed like all the future could hold was more darkness, more depression, & more emptiness. I

24

didn't know how I was going to deal with all of that, unrelenting, year after year. **But now, I feel the deepest confidence & faith in myself that I not only will everything be okay, but I will too because I've become the kind of person now who will always find a way to thrive.**

I am going to keep adding new tools to my toolbox. I will keep searching & seeking & exploring & finding new ones to add to it. Especially when it comes to something as important as mental health, it's vital that you don't become complacent. This is something I will always be tweaking & improving & discovering new things about. I recognize that being cured is still dependent on me building & maintaining the foundation I have built. But I know how.

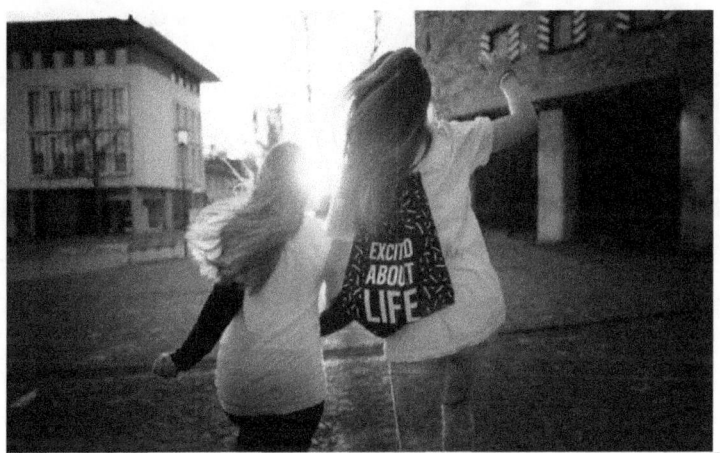
Photo by Kevin Schmia *on* Unsplash

And I'm not saying that I will never feel down again. I assume that at some point, I will. **It's just that I will never let it become part of my personality <u>EVER</u> again.**

Because now, I finally have a sign that I'm heading in the right direction.

I am filled with an expansive playfulness & enthusiasm towards life & towards the kind of future that I can not only build for myself, but use to light the way for others too.

I feel genuinely transformed. Instead of being world-wearied & fearful when I think of the future, I am filled with a deep, unrelenting confidence now. **The confidence that whatever happens, I have the tools & know how to keep being the person who can handle it.**

And I am exceptionally excited to see what comes next.

BOUGHT TODAY

Owl flip flops / Smiley face flip flops /
Wind chime / Polka dot gift bag / whiteboard
for Mom / pumpkin seeds / neon erasers /
water bottle - green / eye drops / felt owl
stickers / owl love you forever wall poster /
Owl wood sculpture / neon highlighters /
Owl mug / motor oil / fruit bowl /
purple glass polka dot cup / marbles /
Garden Chicken sculpture / / / / / / neopoliton
soy ice cream / Chia seed sweet peach
Naked Juice / orange carrot naked juice /
pomegranate lychee green tea / dark chocolate
acai berries / Bolthouse vanilla Chai tea /
Red machine Naked Juice / Sauerkraut /
pretzel sticks / Vegan mayo / green olives /
matzo ball mix / guava nectar / dried banana
chips / Kale / organic carrots / Cranberry
raisin Chocolate trail mix / Cherry Cranberry
raisins / Soba noodles / Taylor Gold
Pear / Tomatillos / Bananas / ginger root /
Persian Lime / Star fruit / blueberries /
peach / white flesh nectarine / pita bread

AFRICAN VIOLET

7-30 2:05

27

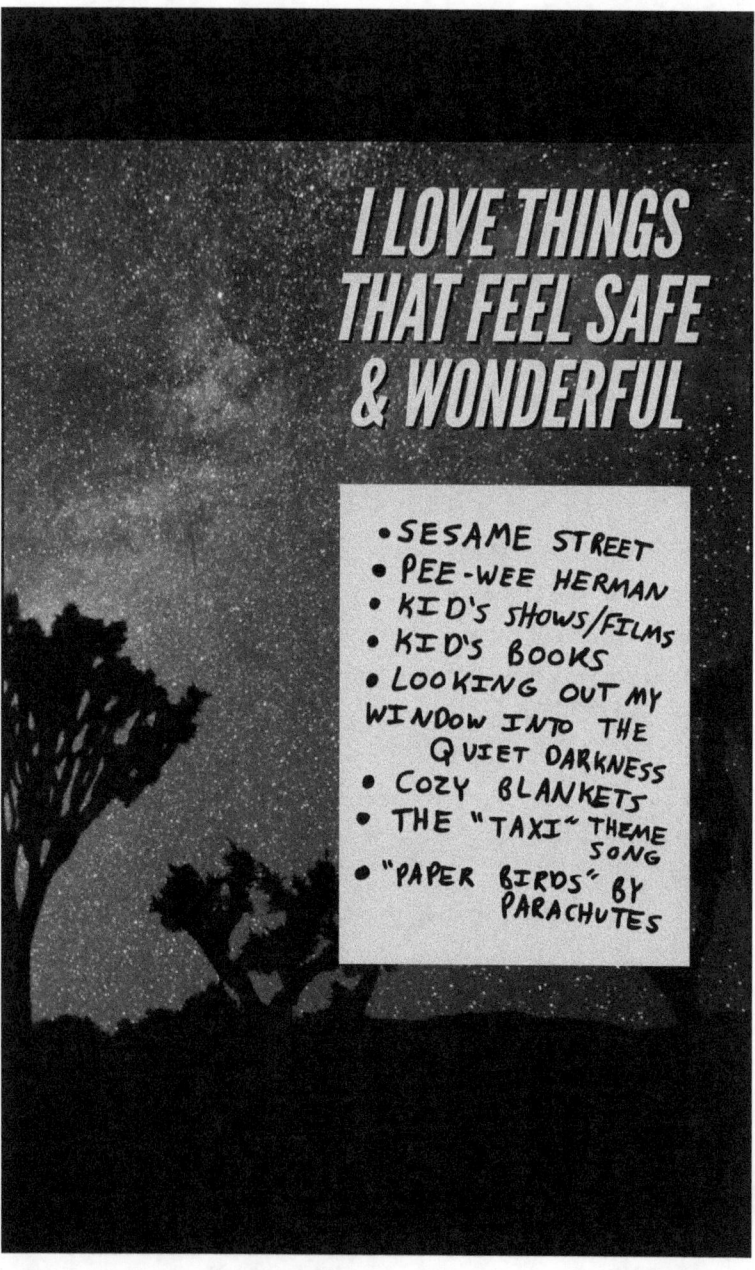

I LOVE THINGS THAT FEEL SAFE & WONDERFUL

- SESAME STREET
- PEE-WEE HERMAN
- KID'S SHOWS/FILMS
- KID'S BOOKS
- LOOKING OUT MY WINDOW INTO THE QUIET DARKNESS
- COZY BLANKETS
- THE "TAXI" THEME SONG
- "PAPER BIRDS" BY PARACHUTES

28

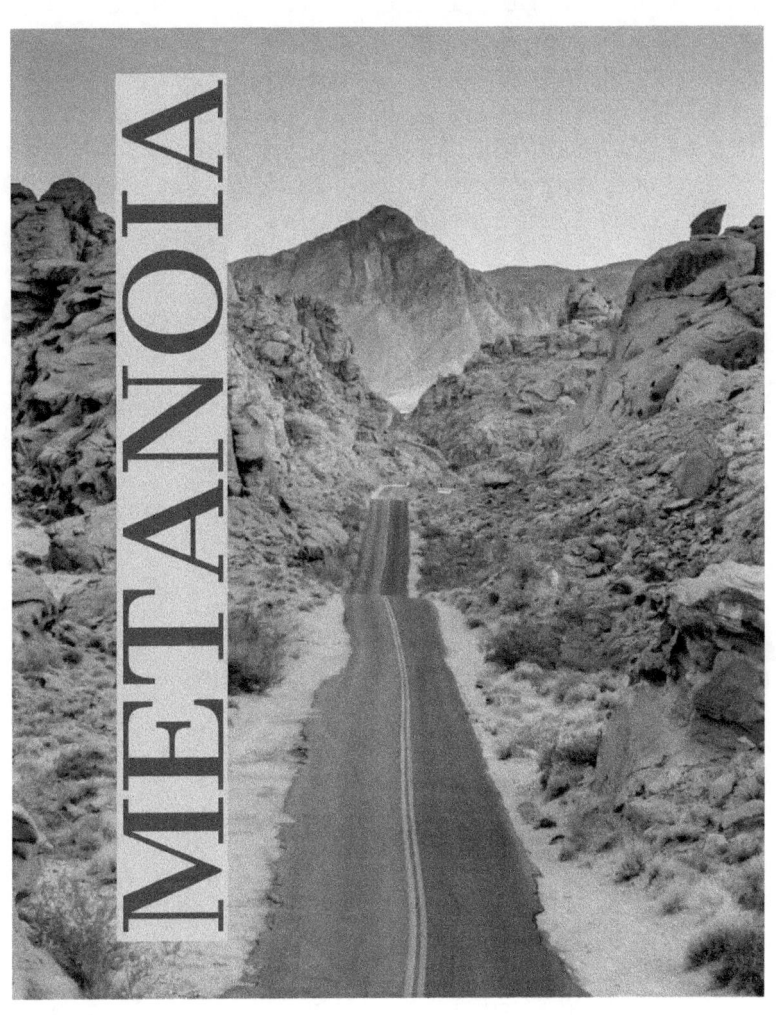

METANOIA

metanoia is "a transformative change of heart". it especially means a spiritual conversion, but i don't think that's necessary. i like the concept of metanoia in general. of having a transformative change of heart, a sudden revelation that changes everything in the best way possible for you. it is a form of joyous reinvention.

how can you experience your own form of metanoia?

10 SIMPLE METANOIA THINGS YOU CAN DO RIGHT NOW:

1. Smile more or try to be the person you've always wanted to.
2. Overcome/find helpful tools/learn to cope better with stress/anxiety/depression.
3. Become more confident in who you are.
4. Become stronger (in any way)
5. Experiment with who you'd like to be.
6. Remain happy (maybe the storm really is over; maybe there is no other shoe)
7. Become an Explorer of the World (a la Keri Smith)
8. Notice more of the things around you; be more mindful/present.
9. Love the little things more. Let the movies & music & books & small things sustain you.
10. Try to make every day as FUN as possible.

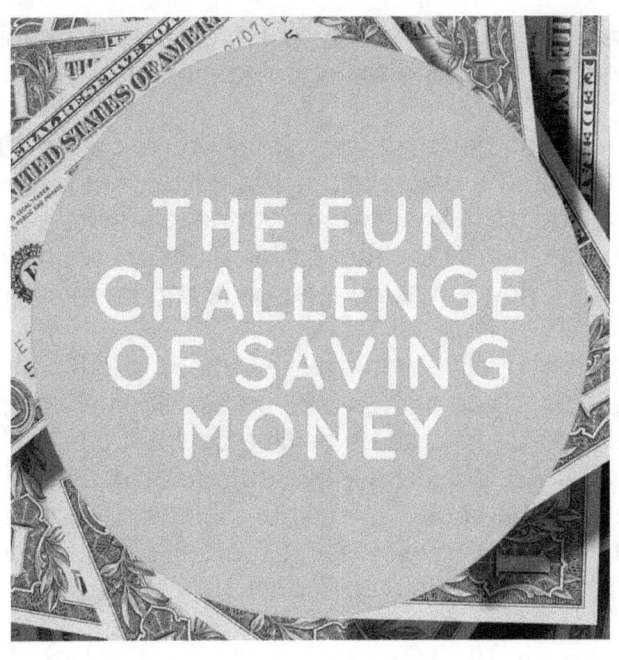

THE FUN
CHALLENGE
OF SAVING
MONEY

Over the past few months, I've read the awesome book "Secrets of the Millionaire Mind" by T. Harv Eker twice. While it's mostly about the acquiring the mindset of a millionaire, it also has what I have been using as a good method for how to divide up your money & increase your net worth.

NOTE: I am not a financial planner or other qualified financial professional. The views expressed here are my own. Please speak with an actual financial planner before making any decisions about finances.

In Secrets of the Millionaire Mind, Eker recommends the reader put 10% of their income into some sort of investment, 10% into long term savings, & use 10% as fun, discretionary income. Obviously you can use any amount you want, but if 10% if affordable, I personally think this is a good methodology for saving money.

This is great, because each week you're taking 20% of your income & using it to increase your net worth. (In case you don't know what your net worth is, a quick Google search for 'how to calculate net worth' will break it down in a way everyone can understand).

What I personally think is even better if you have pesky debt is, if you can, to take an additional 10% (or whatever % - it could be as little as 1% if that's all you can do, but it MUST be a percentage of income & not a set dollar amount, so as your income changes the amount you save/invest in yourself also changes accordingly). Use this additional 10% to pay down your debt.

And, IMO it's time to go Suze Orman on this one & do what she recommends in *The Courage to Be Rich*: pay down your smallest debt (or most pressing) first, then snowball the money you were spending paying down the now-paid-off debt into paying down the second smallest debt, etc. For example, if the minimum payment on one of your credit cards was $50 & you paid this credit card first because it had the smallest balance, once you paid off the credit card you'd take the $50 you were paying each month for Card 1. If Card 2 had a minimum payment of $100 a month, combined with what you were paying but no longer have to pay on Card 1, snowball the money saved from Card 1 & combine it with Card 2 so you could pay $150 a month on Card 2. Check out Suze Orman's books for a deeper understanding of this.

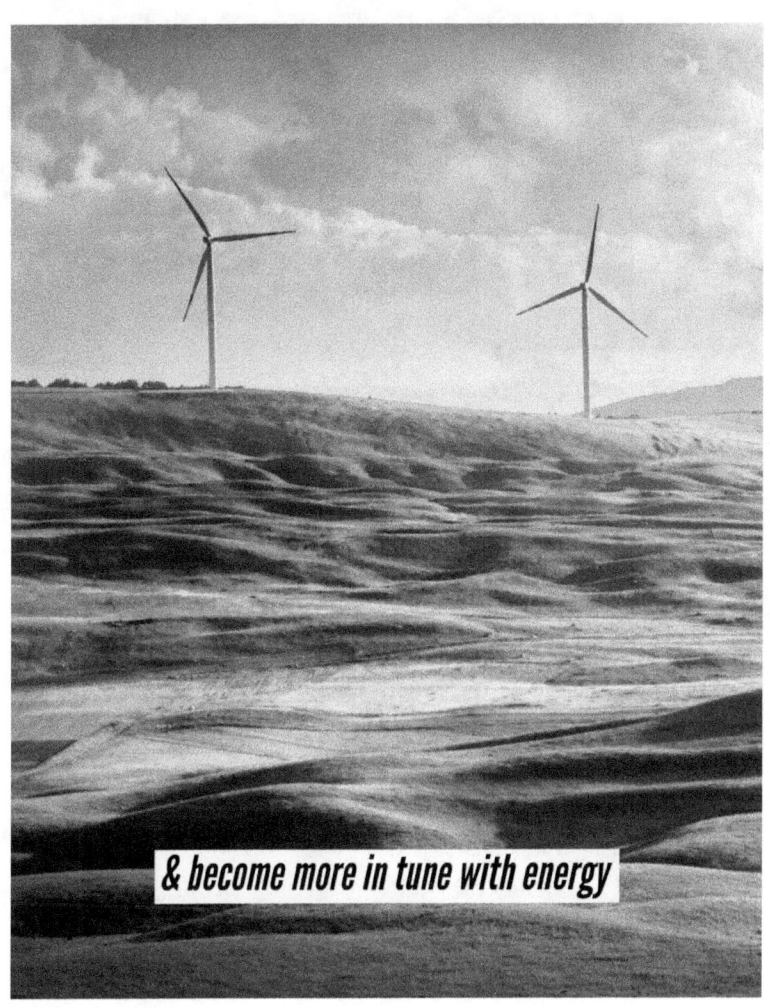

& become more in tune with energy

RHYTHM STICKS

RHYTHM STICKS

BONGO DRUMS

KAZOO

RHYTHM STICKS

COWBELL

BONGO DRUMS

KAZOO

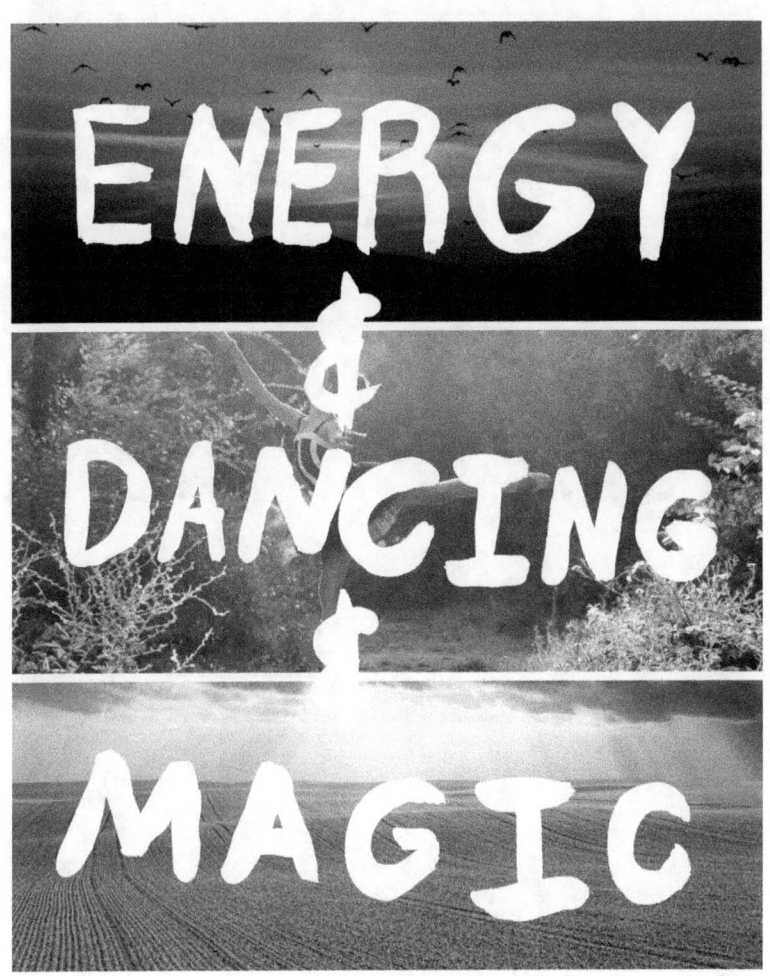

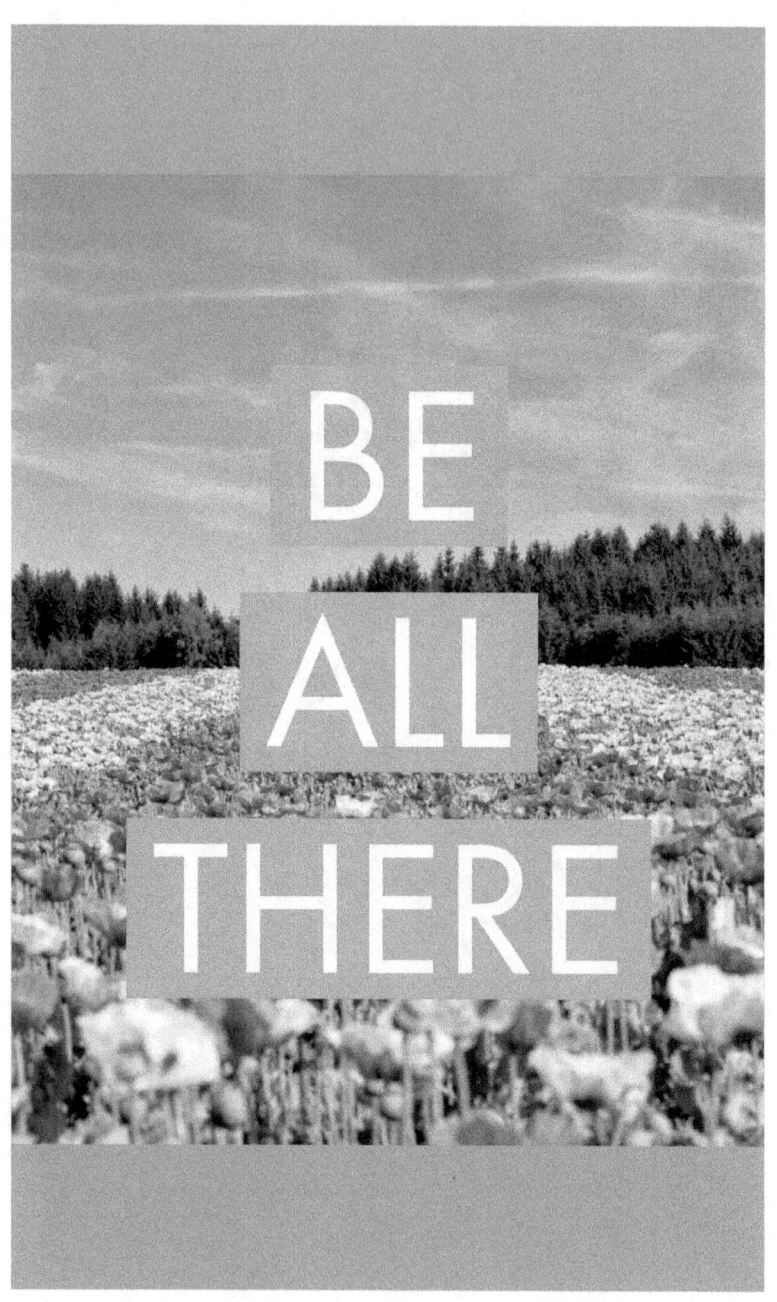

BE
ALL
THERE

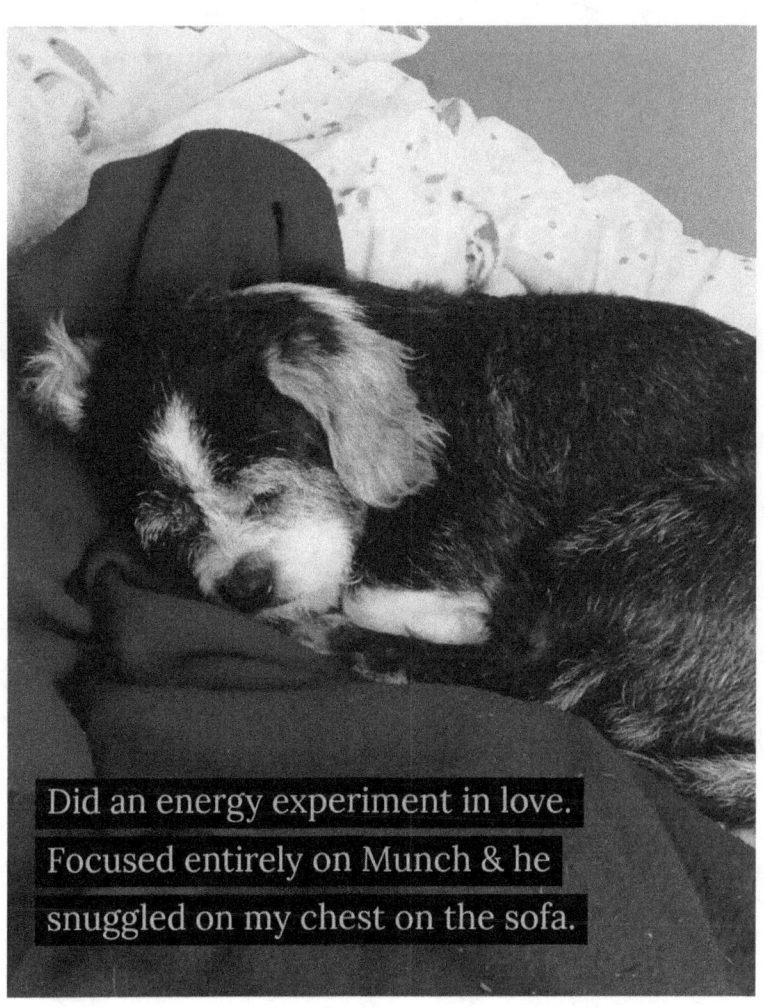

Did an energy experiment in love.
Focused entirely on Munch & he
snuggled on my chest on the sofa.

I'm not getting *depressed,* I'm just kind of *emotional* because of *hormones* -

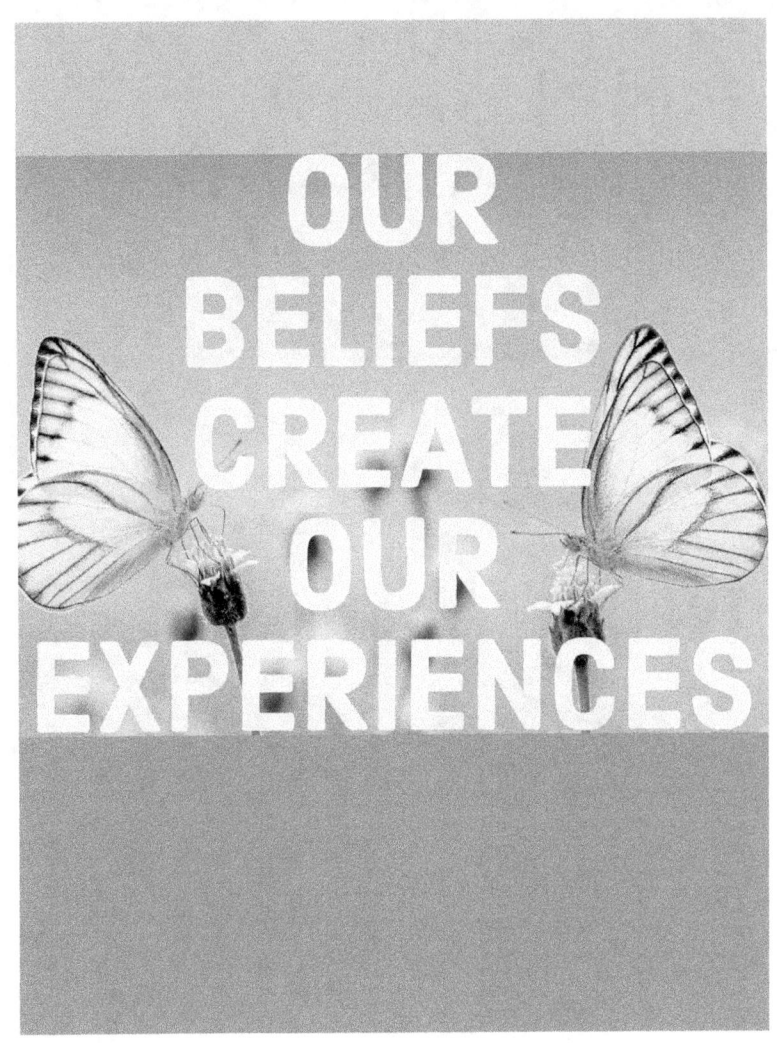

OUR
BELIEFS
CREATE
OUR
EXPERIENCES

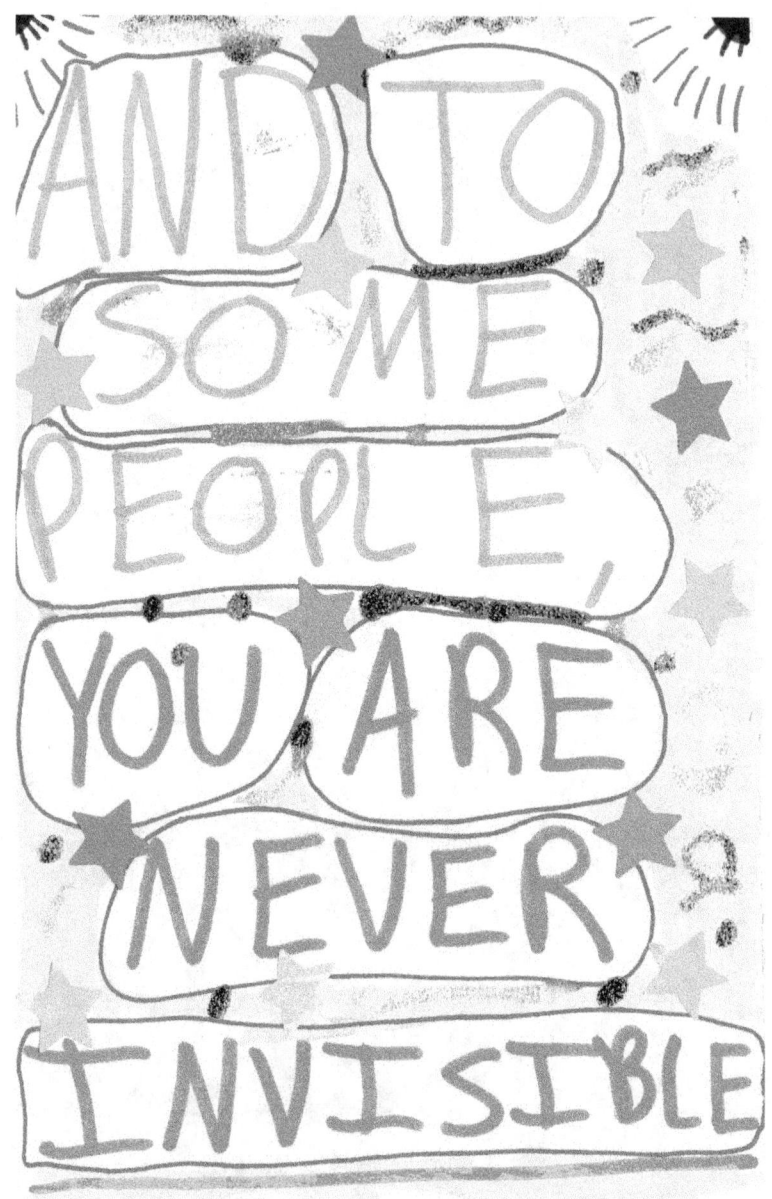

AND TO SOME PEOPLE, YOU ARE NEVER INVISIBLE

INTERVIEW
WITH GUITARIST
PAUL BIELATOWICZ

I am so thrilled that I had the opportunity to interview Paul Bielatowicz, who is one of the best guitarists I've had the chance to see live. I saw him play guitar as part of the Carl Palmer's ELP Legacy concert I attended in 2018 & was immediately impressed. Paul manages to combine a killer virtuoso technique with truly beautiful, evocative playing, which can be a challenging combination to find. Paul pulls it off perfectly, & I'm so grateful that I got to pick his brain about music & creativity.

1. Is creating music something you HAVE to & feel a deep & necessary compulsion to do? Has being such a creative person sometimes made your life more difficult/painful or less fun, because being very creative is often at odds with what the rest of the world wants from you? If so, how have you dealt with that? Or has this been easy overall?

I've not really thought about it in those terms before, but I've always felt a deep need to be creative. I wouldn't be happy if I wasn't doing something creative with my life. Thankfully I've never felt at odds because of it; in fact the opposite is true, being creative has brought so many great people into my life.

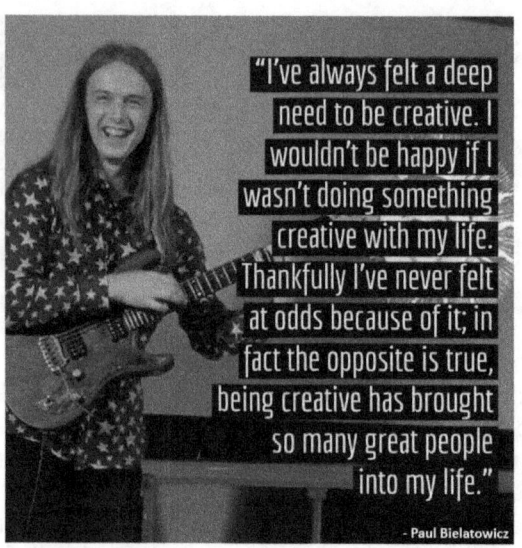

"I've always felt a deep need to be creative. I wouldn't be happy if I wasn't doing something creative with my life. Thankfully I've never felt at odds because of it; in fact the opposite is true, being creative has brought so many great people into my life."

- Paul Bielatowicz

2. How did you end up playing as part of Carl Palmer's ELP Legacy? Did you have to audition? (If you did, what song(s) did you play?) Tell us that story.

Carl was looking for a guitarist and asked around for recommendations. One of his recommendations was a guitarist called Guthrie Govan – he couldn't do it because of other commitments, so Guthrie kindly recommended me. I sent Carl a CD of demos I had recorded – he liked it, so asked me to join the band. Thankfully there was no audition, the first time I met him was the first of 3 days rehearsals before our first European tour.

3. Do you consider yourself an explorer of the world (particularly the music world) or a collector of experiences & ideas, which you then turn into sounds? What things outside of music

influence you, even including random things in the everyday world?

I think everything you experience goes into and comes out of your music. My goal is always to communicate something when I play or create music, so obviously it's very important to have something to communicate. Inspiration can come from many places, but for me I try to communicate the positive in my music, simply because that's what I'm drawn toward. So any positive experience or emotion can be inspiration for music.

4. Do you feel that playfulness & fun are important themes in your life & your music, & are taking creative risks a form of play? Do you have fun being yourself? How can creative people integrate more playfulness & creative fun into their lives/creative work?

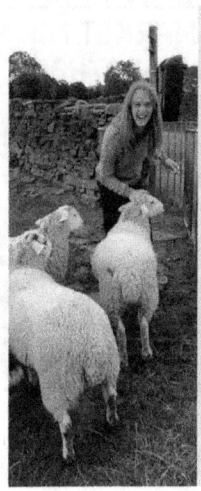

"I think fun and silliness is a big part of who I am, so that's naturally going to come out in my music. If I can make someone smile, or even laugh, when I performing then I feel like I've done my job. As for how people can integrate more playfulness - if you're that way inclined then just be yourself. An audience appreciates honesty in a performer."

- Paul Bielatowicz

Absolutely. I think fun and silliness is a big part of who I am, so that's naturally going to come out in my music. If I can make someone smile, or even laugh, when I performing then I feel like I've done my job. As for how people can integrate more playfulness – if you're that way inclined then just be yourself. An audience appreciates honesty in a performer.

5. Are most of the solos you play planned out or improvised, & why?

I'll usually improvise solos in the studio until I get a take that I like, then when I'm happy with it I'll keep it and play it live that way pretty much all the time.

6. What have you found to be the best way to market your music?

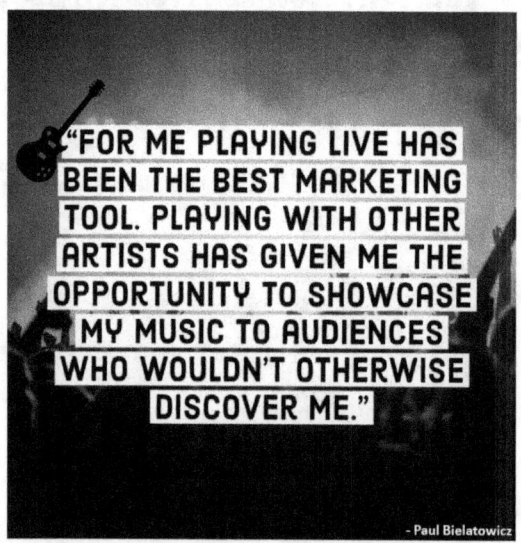

"FOR ME PLAYING LIVE HAS BEEN THE BEST MARKETING TOOL. PLAYING WITH OTHER ARTISTS HAS GIVEN ME THE OPPORTUNITY TO SHOWCASE MY MUSIC TO AUDIENCES WHO WOULDN'T OTHERWISE DISCOVER ME."

- Paul Bielatowicz

For me playing live has been the best marketing tool. Playing with other artists has given me the opportunity to showcase my music to audiences who wouldn't otherwise discover me.

7. When you are writing a song, how do you know what it should sound like? Can you hear, feel, or see what the parts should be like inside your mind? Do you try to use sound to "paint" a very specific feeling or aesthetic you have in mind, or something else?

There's no fixed formula for me – the writing process happens differently every time. I just wrote a song include 132 names of my Patreon patrons in the lyrics. The morning I found out my patron count had passed 100 subscribers I got in the shower and pretty much had the whole thing written by the time I got out. Then I sang it into my phone so I could remember it. Other times I've been commissioned by guitar magazines to write pieces in a very specific style; in those instances I usually try to find an existing piece of music to use as a model for the piece I'm writing. In terms of the aesthetic or meaning of a piece sometimes the musical idea comes first, and that might bring to mind a feeling or narrative to mind, and the rest of the piece is then influenced by that narrative... and it can also happen the other way round. So, for me, there's no tried and tested method for writing.

8. If you could have written or played on any album (or albums!), which would it be & why? What would you have done differently on it?

Great question! I'm thinking of all my favourite albums, but the problem is they're perfect exactly how they are, so I wouldn't want to change them by adding myself. Having said that, I would have loved to have been in the studio when Sgt. Pepper or Abbey Road was being recorded – that creative environment must have been been something incredible to witness.

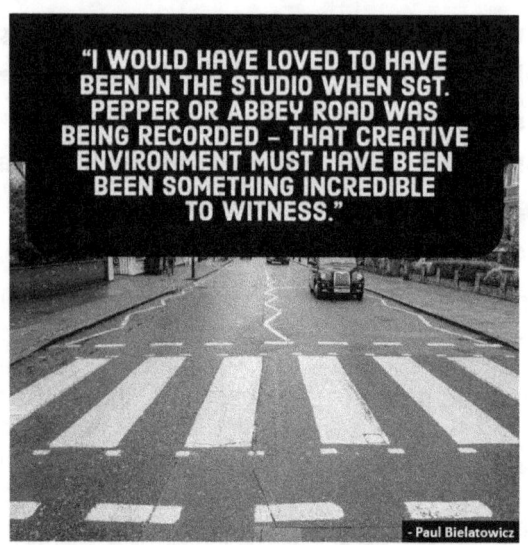

"I WOULD HAVE LOVED TO HAVE BEEN IN THE STUDIO WHEN SGT. PEPPER OR ABBEY ROAD WAS BEING RECORDED – THAT CREATIVE ENVIRONMENT MUST HAVE BEEN BEEN SOMETHING INCREDIBLE TO WITNESS."

- Paul Bielatowicz

9. Who are some of your biggest musical influences & what most appeals to you about their music? How have they inspired your approach to guitar?

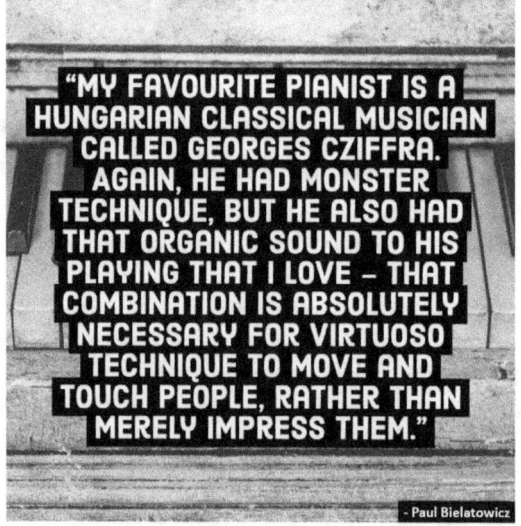

"MY FAVOURITE PIANIST IS A HUNGARIAN CLASSICAL MUSICIAN CALLED GEORGES CZIFFRA. AGAIN, HE HAD MONSTER TECHNIQUE, BUT HE ALSO HAD THAT ORGANIC SOUND TO HIS PLAYING THAT I LOVE – THAT COMBINATION IS ABSOLUTELY NECESSARY FOR VIRTUOSO TECHNIQUE TO MOVE AND TOUCH PEOPLE, RATHER THAN MERELY IMPRESS THEM."

- Paul Bielatowicz

Guitar-wise, I started playing guitar because of Mark Knopfler from Dire Straits. Then I discovered Hendrix & Eddie Van Halen and my life changed. With Eddie & Jimi, what really appeals is the organic sound and style of playing – they sound so "human" when they play. One thing I dislike is when a musician, particularly guitar players, sound mechanical & robot-like. Aside from guitar players, a huge influence has been piano music. My favourite pianist is a Hungarian classical musician called Georges Cziffra. Again, he had monster technique, but he also had that organic sound to his playing that I love – that combination is absolutely necessary for virtuoso technique to move and touch people, rather than merely impress them.

10. With someone as virtuosic at guitar as you are, how do you know where to take your playing next? Do you have a mentor or a teacher, people you look up to & aspire to be like, or does the "next level" of honing your skills come from intuition or trying to play what you might hear inside your mind?

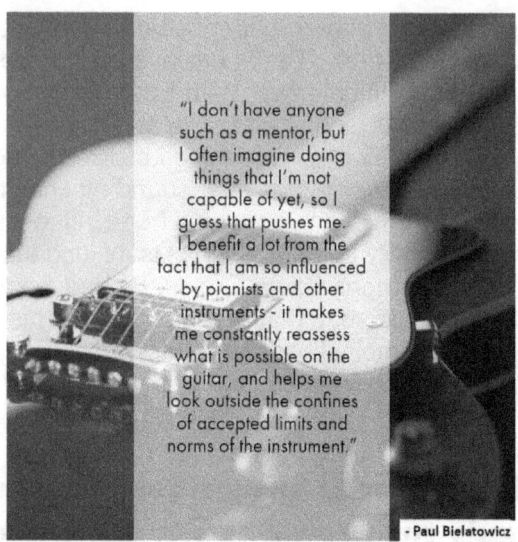

"I don't have anyone such as a mentor, but I often imagine doing things that I'm not capable of yet, so I guess that pushes me. I benefit a lot from the fact that I am so influenced by pianists and other instruments - it makes me constantly reassess what is possible on the guitar, and helps me look outside the confines of accepted limits and norms of the instrument."

- Paul Bielatowicz

I don't have anyone such as a mentor, but I often imagine doing things that I'm not capable of yet, so I guess that pushes me. I benefit a lot from the fact that I am so influenced by pianists and other instruments – it makes me constantly reassess what is possible on the guitar, and helps me look outside the confines of accepted limits and norms of the instrument.

11. If you had to write a manifesto about your approach to life in the form of a five-item list, what would that list be?

1. Be kind.
2. Be original.
3. Create.
4. Make the most of every moment.
5. Leave the world a better place than you found it.

12. Do you have any hobbies outside of music? Tell us about your "son" (aka your cat!).

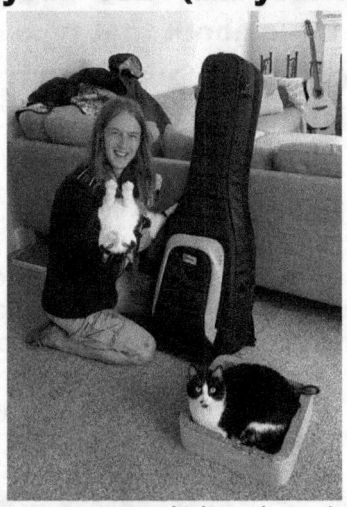

I adopted a cat from a rescue shelter about 4 years ago. We went to the shelter wanting a cat to pick us, rather than the other way round. The shelter let us meet a few cats, but they all seemed mainly interested in getting treats... then we met one who the shelter had called Rhode Island (that's where he was rescued from) – there was an instant bond between us. He wasn't interested in any treats, but followed us around the room whenever we walked away from him. He acted more like a dog than a cat, so we decided to call him Darwin – we figured he was the missing evolutionary link between a cat and a dog! 6 months later we read a heart wrenching story about a cat who had been in the same shelter for a long time; she came from Rhode Island and all her siblings had been adopted months ago; we called the shelter and sure enough it was Darwin's biological sister, so obviously we had to reunite them. We named her Emma, after Charles Darwin's wife, Emma Darwin.

13. I love the collaborative combos you make by combining a silent film with your guitar. What is your favorite thing about that type of combination of taking something from the past & combining it with the present?Tell us about that process.

I've always liked the idea of working with multimedia, so when the idea of silent movies came up, it just seemed to tick all the boxes. They're a blank canvas – no dialog or existing soundtrack to get in the way of the music I'm playing, they're often pieces of art in the their own right (we could dedicate a whole other interview to that idea alone!) and what's more, they're now in the public domain so can be used freely without worrying about the treading minefield of copyright!

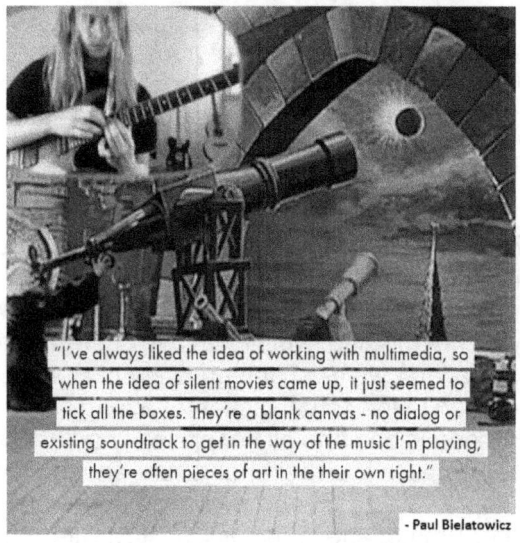

"I've always liked the idea of working with multimedia, so when the idea of silent movies came up, it just seemed to tick all the boxes. They're a blank canvas - no dialog or existing soundtrack to get in the way of the music I'm playing, they're often pieces of art in the their own right."

- Paul Bielatowicz

14. What's the earliest memory you have of music being important to you? Were you always interested in music & becoming a musician, or was that something you developed over time (if so, when & what inspired you to come to that decision?). If you hadn't done something with music, what might have you become or done?

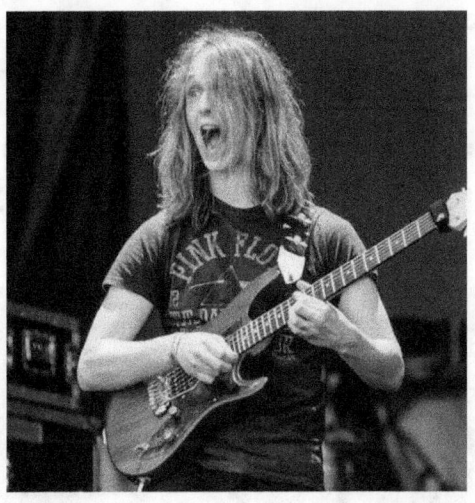

I was an only child growing up on the outskirts of a small country village so when music became important to me in my teen years, it became REALLY important – I threw myself into it and it consumed my every thought. When I was at school I loved playing guitar, but never thought it was a viable career choice so didn't dare tell anyone I wanted to be a musician in case they laughed at me! Then when it came time to chose what to study at college I had a kind of "now or never" moment – it was the closest I'd been to choosing what I wanted to do with the rest of my life, so I finally started telling people I wanted to study music. Thankfully my family were very supportive and the rest is history!

15. What is an unusual habit or absurd thing that you love?

Geocaching! Me and Simon (Fitzpatrick – the bass player in Carl Palmer's band) take part in a worldwide treasure hunt called Geocaching. There are millions of "caches" hidden all over the world – basically small containers containing a log book for you to sign – and we always try to find as many as we can on our travels.

16. Do you ever pretend to be someone else or do you feel as though you are always entirely yourself? Do you ever pretend to be your heroes when you're up on stage, or does it feel amazing to always be exactly who you are when you're on stage?

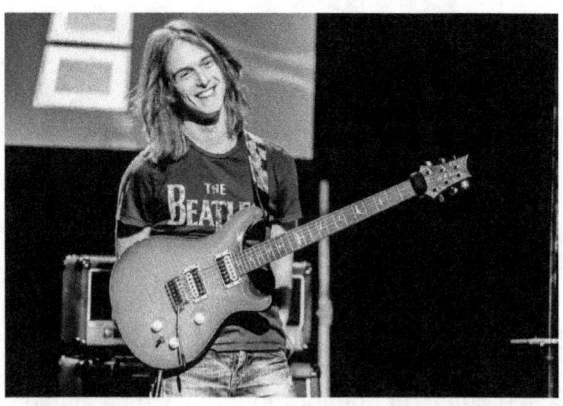

Haha no, definitely always feel like I'm entirely myself. I think my approach to performing is a very personal, communication-based one. So I'm always trying to draw the audience into to the performance and communicate something to them. I don't think I'd feel comfortable trying to pretend to be someone else as that would lose the element of communication.

17. You can commission a work of art in any medium (including music & film) by any artist, dead or alive. Who is it, & what do you have them make for you?

Beethoven – I'd get him to compose me an electric guitar concerto!

18. Did you have a "point of no return" experience in regards to pursing music, where there was no turning back & you knew you were just going to go for it? What was that decision or moment, & how did it make you feel?

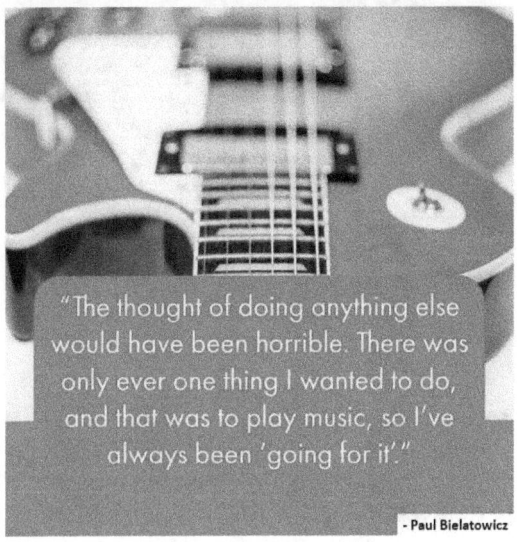

"The thought of doing anything else would have been horrible. There was only ever one thing I wanted to do, and that was to play music, so I've always been 'going for it'."

- Paul Bielatowicz

Not really. The thought of doing anything else would have been horrible. There was only ever one thing I wanted to do, and that was to play music, so I've always been "going for it".

53

19. In the last five years, what new belief, behavior, or habit, has most improved your life?

I decided to go vegan a few years ago and I feel like I'm a better person for it. I reached a point where I felt I had to reassess my moral compass and make my own decisions about what was right and wrong. A big influence was adopting Darwin, my cat from a rescue centre – it was the first time I'd really bonded with an animal and all of a sudden the thought that I'd been eating animals really struck home. I realised I had to make that change in my life & I've never looked back. Going vegan is one of the most positive things I've ever done with my life.

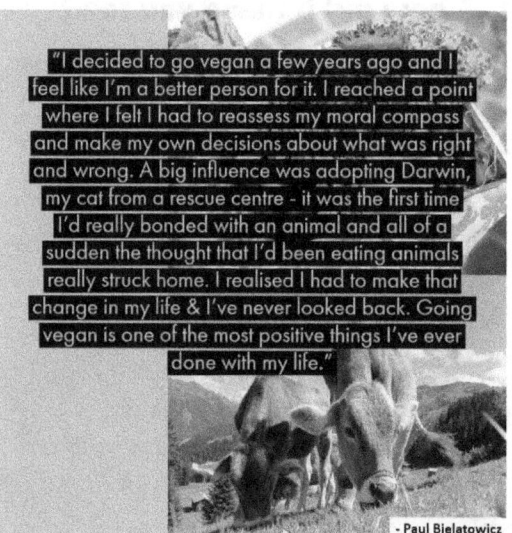

- Paul Bielatowicz

20. What advice do you have for highly creative & eclectic young people pursuing their art?

Be yourself. The world doesn't need a clone of any other artist out there. Find your own artistic voice and create.

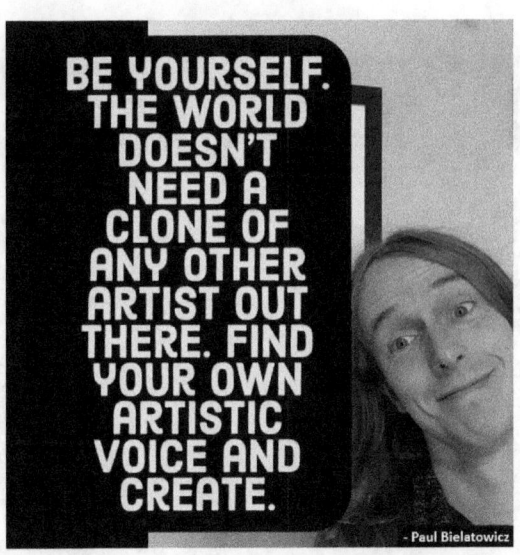

BE YOURSELF. THE WORLD DOESN'T NEED A CLONE OF ANY OTHER ARTIST OUT THERE. FIND YOUR OWN ARTISTIC VOICE AND CREATE.

- Paul Bielatowicz

If you'd like to keep up with what Paul is up to in the studio or on tour, they can check out www.patreon.com/paulbielatowicz for daily updates.

You can also find Paul on <u>Facebook</u> at https://www.facebook.com/paulbguitar/.

All photos of Paul from his Facebook page.

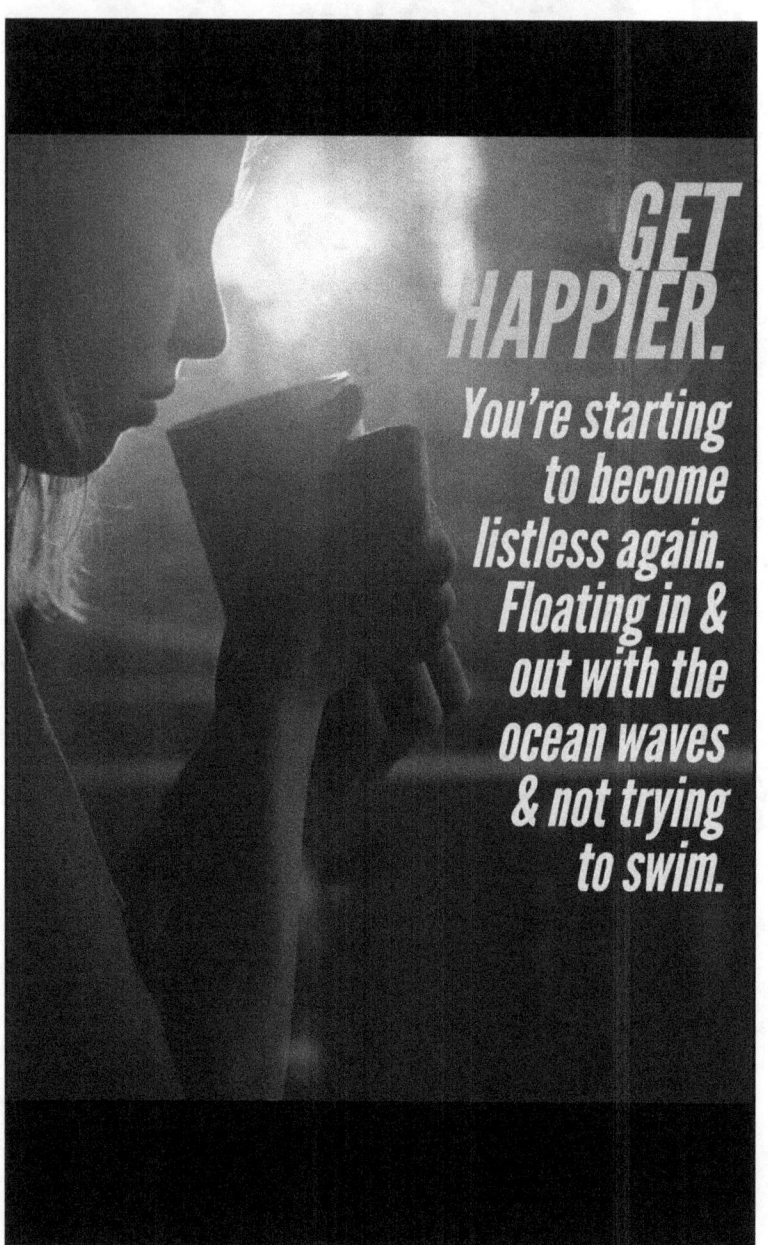

GET HAPPIER.

You're starting to become listless again. Floating in & out with the ocean waves & not trying to swim.

DON'T LET IT DULL YOUR SOUL

"I'M STARTING TO HAVE A VERY GOOD FEELING ABOUT TODAY."

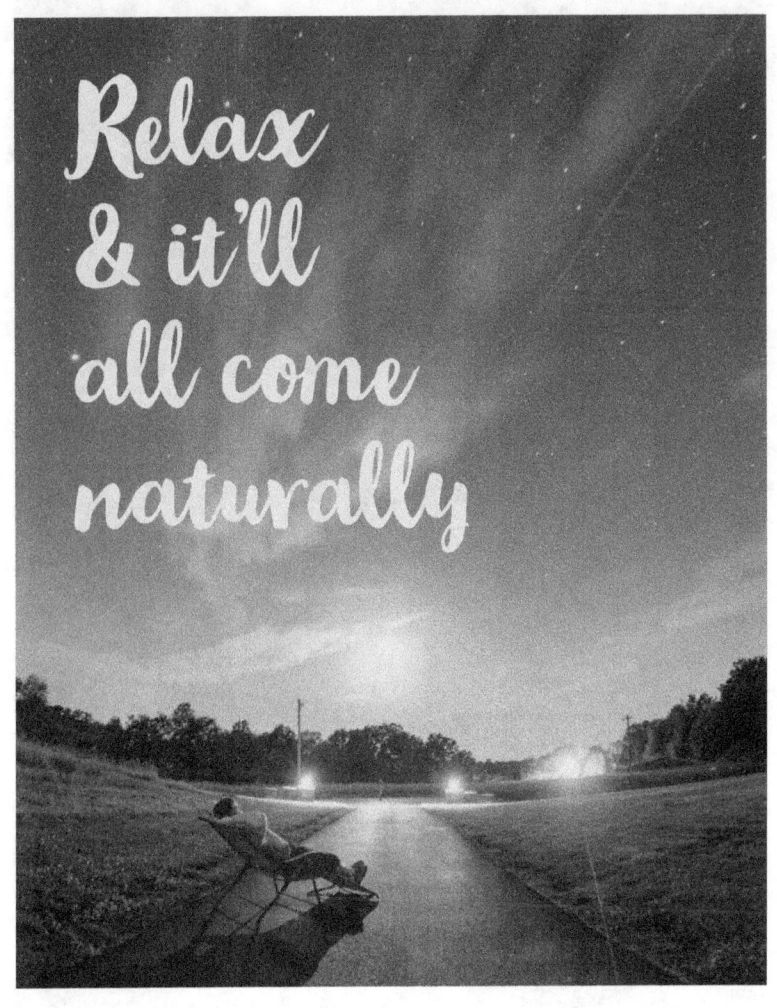

Relax & it'll all come naturally

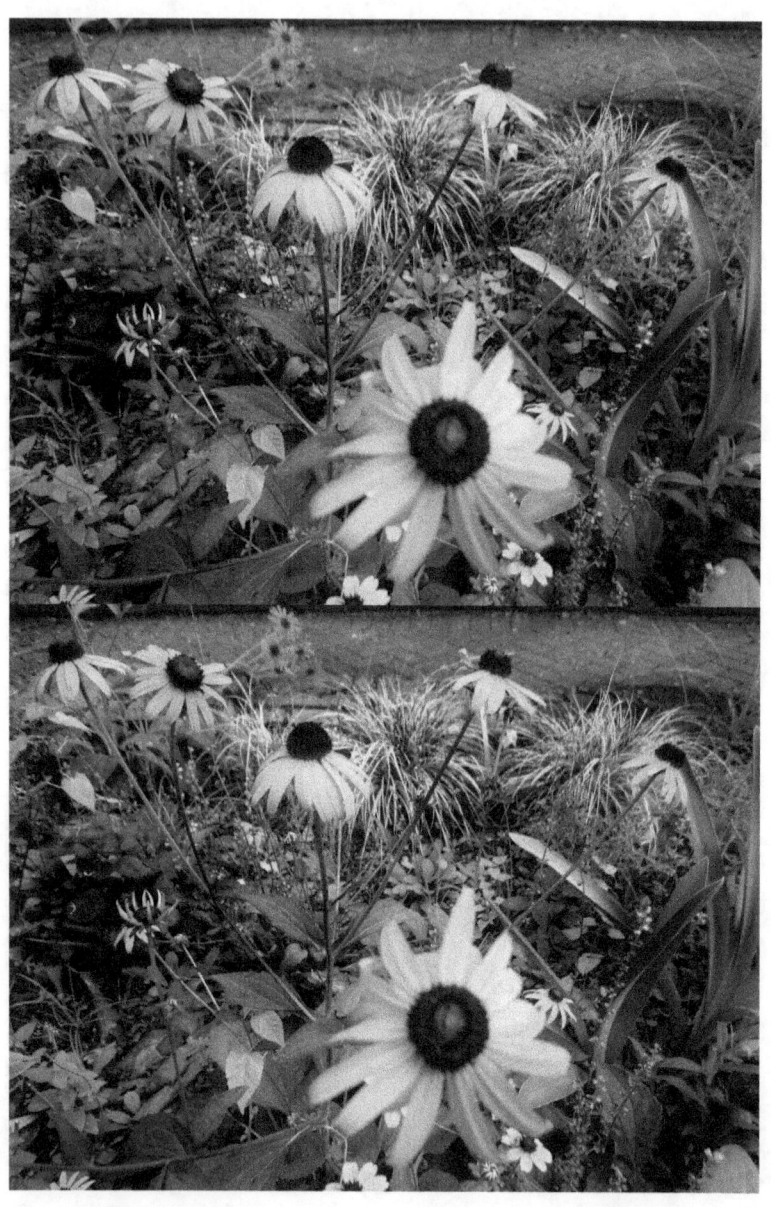

Last year I cried because I promised myself
that by this time next year, I would be okay.
I would have won. I would finally be happy.
I would have everything that I needed. A
kind, friendly, supportive group of people
who cared about me & made me feel like
it was okay to be who I was, a group who
empowered me to be my best self & loved
me for who I was. At the time I promised
myself that, I did not see any way that it
could happen. It seemed impossible. But
I still promised myself that, vowed that to
myself over & over again, that somehow
& some way, I would be the person I'd
always wanted to be. That I would be happy.
Well, this year, things are different.
This year, I've made it.
This year, I have done it. I've done the
impossible.
I am so happy now.
& it feels so beautiful.

MAKE
POWERFUL
GOALS

THE UNIVERSE IS TROLLING ON YOUR BEHALF

THE UNIVERSE IS TROLLING ON YOUR BEHALF

THE UNIVERSE
IS TROLLING
ON YOUR
BEHALF

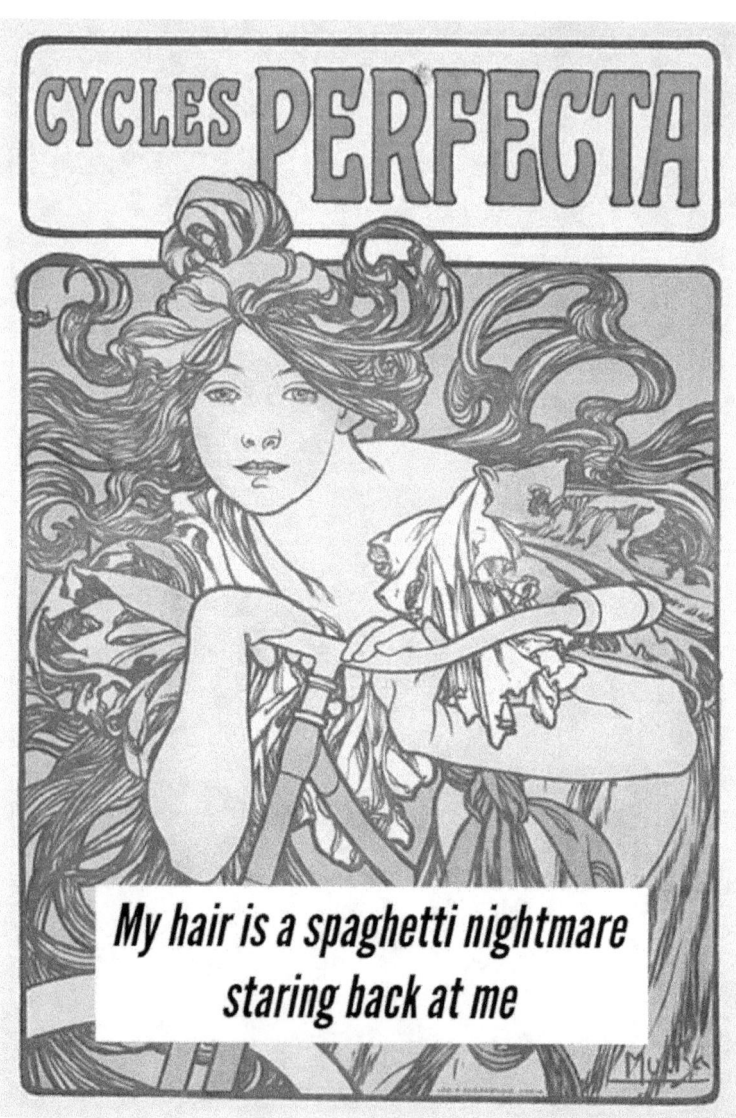

CYCLES PERFECTA

My hair is a spaghetti nightmare staring back at me

About the Author

Ashlee Craft is an author, poet, musician, artist, filmmaker, & photographer. She has written more than 60 books in a variety of genres, & publishes an art & poetry zine called Assemblage. Ashlee is also the CEO of the publishing company Freedom Meadow Media, owns an online store called SHOP Ashlee Craft. She can be found writing on her blog, Ashlee Craft's World, creating art, playing with her menagerie of pets, & living by her life-is-a-playground motto.

www.ingramcontent.com/pod-product-compliance
Lightning Source LLC
Chambersburg PA
CBHW072206170526
45158CB00004BB/1780